In the Suffering

Jodie Mitchell

IN THE SUFFERING

Copyright © 2012 Jodie Mitchell.
All rights reserved. No part of this publication's content may
be reproduced, stored in a retrieval system, or transmitted in any
form or by any means---electronic, mechanical, photocopy, recording,
or any other---without the prior permission of the Author.
Unless otherwise indicated, all Scripture references are from
THE HOLY BIBLE, NEW INTERNATIONAL VERSION®,
NIV® Copyright © 1973, 1978, 1984, 2011 by Biblica, Inc.™
Used by permission.

All rights reserved worldwide.

ISBN: 1467914274
ISBN-13: 978-1467914277

Published in the United States of America
by April Sky Ministries

"Be still, and know that I am God..."
Psalm 46:10

DEDICATION

If you or your loved ones have ever
known suffering from crippling trials,
chronic illness, or constant sorrow in this life...
this book is prayerfully dedicated to you.

May the poems in this book offer you His Peace,
His Encouragement, and His Strength.

*Be joyful in hope, patient
in affliction, faithful in prayer.
Romans 12:12*

IN THE SUFFERING

In The Suffering

Today as I awakened,
The pain would not go away...

So, I struggled to find some strength,
And face the routine day.

On most mornings it's hard to ignore...
Such pain and misery.

And though some days are bearable,
The pain is there constantly.

Still...

I will seek out a place of refuge,
A place of Peace for me...

When I meet with my Loving Savior,
In quiet company.

I will open up the pages of His Word,
And all its many treasures.

I will sing a song of Praise,
Of His love which can't be measured.

And then when He lifts me up,
His Presence will fill my soul.

Because in Him I find everything,
He is in complete control.

So today I will remember His Truth,
And the Promise that His Word brings...

For He is with me every hour,
Even in the suffering.

IN THE SUFFERING

TABLE OF CONTENTS

	Dedication	iv
	Acknowledgments	ix
	Message from the Author	x
Section One	Drowning Faith	1
Section Two	Disguised Blessing	23
Section Three	Dark Hours	45
Section Four	Divine Hope	67
	An Invitation for You	85
	Personal Reflections from Your Own Journey	87
	Verses to Cling to	113
	(P.S.,)	117
	Alphabetical Index of Poems	122
	About the Author	124
	Words of Encouragement from Family and Friends	125

IN THE SUFFERING

Acknowledging His Holiness

Thou Lord, You are so great and I am so small,
Though You came to earth humble,
You are Holiest of all.

When I think of how Holy You are,
I realize just who I am,
For I'm so unclean with sin, unto the Worthy Lamb.

My corrupt body of disgrace,
leaves me with nowhere to run,
When Thy illuminating Light shines upon me,
and reveals how I'm undone.

For I live on this earth with sin
and so I must be purged clean,
Before I can face my Lord and Holy King.

So create in me a clean heart Lord,
and show me what to do,
For Father, I know that one day,
I want to be like You.

ACKNOWLEDGMENTS

I would like to personally
thank my dream team:

Phil Mitchell - my husband
For all his hard work, time,
computer expertise and the
photos on pages xii, 66, and 124

Emily Young - my niece
For all her beautiful photography
on pages vi, 22, 44 and cover

Julia Richardson - my dear friend
For all her incredible talent and
artistry with her heavenly illustrations

Message from the Author

In the fall of 2009 I was diagnosed with a chronic condition known as fibromyalgia. At first it was very mild but over time it changed.

I could share about how it has affected my life in many ways and often prevents me from doing the things I love. I could also describe in detail what a good day and what a bad day is like for me with this condition.

However, I would rather tell you about what God has taught me about Himself and who He is in me.

I have learned in my suffering that whether in pain or grief, it isn't about the condition, disease or illness. It's also not about the patient or the doctor, and this may surprise you, but it isn't even about the physical healing.

It *is* about Jesus being visible in my life so that others can see Him as my Hope and see that He is the Answer for their life.

You see, Jesus Himself has already gone before us and understands our trials, pain and grief. He experienced it all with His journey to the cross for you and me.

Furthermore, because He arose from the grave and defeated death, He conquered the Dark Hours at Calvary – so that we could experience Divine Hope for all Eternity. For us, that Hope begins the moment He becomes our Savior. I pray He becomes YOUR Hope as well!

It is for this reason and purpose that I believe God first placed "In the Suffering" as a poem in my previous book, "The Trusting Time - A Collection of Christian Poetry", so He could now manifest it into an entire book of its own.

Therefore, I have included a variety of older poems along with a number of new ones here in this condensed and softer format so as to minister direct encouragement during suffering.

IN THE SUFFERING

To begin, there are four sections of poems which deal with moments of life such as troubles, sickness, grief and hope. Each section, poem, photo and illustration have been strategically placed in a particular order that will serve as a reminder that Jesus wants to be our Sustainer, Healer, Comforter and Eternal Joy.

You will find at the end of each section an encouraging verse along with a prayer from me to you and a special area of bible verses in the back of the book that will calm your heart during the unsettling moments.

I have included a section, *"Personal Reflections for Your Own Journey"* to enhance the healing process as God comforts you during this time. There is also a section, *"Words of Encouragement from Friends and Family"* where those you know may have the opportunity to write a personal message for you.

In conclusion, may I say that I do not know the pain and suffering you or your loved one could be going through and I do not know if you are reading this right now from a comfortable couch, a sick bed in a hospital, or a dimly lit room after a funeral...

However, I do know that there is another Presence with you now and He wants YOU to see Him in the midst of YOUR problems, illness and sorrow.

So go ahead, let God hold you tight.
Just give everything to Him!
Then read these poems and listen close...
for you might just hear the rustle of angel's wings...
because angels are in the Presence of Jesus
and HE is present with YOU now... *even in the suffering*.

Jodie Mitchell

IN THE SUFFERING

But when he saw the wind, he was afraid and, beginning to sink, cried out, "Lord, save me!" Immediately Jesus reached out his hand and caught him. "You of little faith," he said, "why did you doubt?" And when they climbed into the boat, the wind died down. Then those who were in the boat worshiped him, saying, "Truly you are the Son of God." Matthew 14:30-33

IN THE SUFFERING

Section One
Drowning Faith

IN THE SUFFERING

Drowning Faith

One summer, while vacationing with friends...
I was splashing in the ocean during a long days end.
The sun was hot and the waves were blue,
But, with what awaited me, I had not a clue...
I was falling back into the waves, one by one,
As they crashed into the shore, I was having so much fun,

Until they grew stronger and I began to have my doubts,
When I realized the danger, the waves had taken me out...
Into the darkened waters that enveloped me,
In a thick black, blanket of insecurity,
I panicked and started kicking my feet, trying hard to swim ashore,
But my strength was fading fast and the sea had so much more...

A friend tried to save me but I weighed him down...
It hit me in that moment, dear God – I'm going to drown!
After I went under for a third time, I had to finally admit...
There would be no rescue for me, and this was probably it.
I began sinking even deeper, into the emptiness...
And I felt myself starting, to lose consciousness.

Until all at once, I saw a blade of Light, suddenly break through...
It split the gloom beneath and the waves above withdrew...
I wasn't sure what was happening, I couldn't comprehend,
But somehow, I found myself atop the waves again,
And at this very moment my eyes looked out to see,
A lifeguard swimming fast so he could rescue me.

DROWNING FAITH

The only reason I share this story and have lived to tell the tale,
Is because there is a Savior who can calm the stormy gale.
For I know my life was spared and saved many years ago,
By the Hand of God that reached for me and will not let me go.
The moment in the ocean, was my wake-up call,
To see my purpose on this earth and share His Truth with all.

Even though there are some, who may not have escaped life's harm...
For those who know Christ, they are in His Loving arms.
But if you are reading this right now, this is written just for YOU,
Your life may feel over, still this journey continues.
Let me encourage you, with my life and death experience,
God is still there, even when life doesn't make sense.

Our day to day situations, can be hit and miss,
Taking us out further into the dark abyss,
Covering us with pain, heartaches and grief,
Leaving us powerless with little relief.
But the misery, the hard times are all in accord,
To help us draw closer and lean on the Lord.

So, what we must see and try to understand,
Is that drowning faith can sometimes, be a part of God's Plan.
And it's in these times when we will learn, that nothing else can offer,
A safer place to be or tread... than with Jesus on the water.

IN THE SUFFERING

Storms of Life

Last night the storms that beat my window sill,
And had thundered all around,
Were the same storms that beat the weeds,
Yet sprung flowers from the ground.

The lightening that brightened the night,
And struck in the sky,
Also reassured my faith,
That God was close by.

The rain that fell for hours,
That I felt lasted so long,
Provided drinks for little birds,
That would sing His morning song.

So I got down beside my bed,
And I fell down on my knees,
In prayer I praised Him for the rain,
And for His inner peace...

For that is when I realized...

It's in the storms of life, when we should come to know,
That God is only watering us, for His sunshine,
That will someday help us GROW!

Sand Castles

Children running along the beach, beside the ocean's shore,
Making castles out of sand, till the sun shines no more.
But the tide that rolls in at night will erase their art...
Which had been carefully put into place, made from their heart.
No matter how much work was done, through the course of that day,
The tide will always return, and remove their creation all away.

In life our dreams are like sand castles, that we build so high...
As we try to accomplish our goals, while reaching for the sky.
The changes in life that surprise us, always come around,
Breaking our world into pieces, causing it to fall down.

So we begin to lose touch with God, because of our fear,
And our trust in Him seems to fail, as we watch it disappear.
But we should let go of the temporary, and all life's tide has destroyed,
And focus on whatever is eternal, so God can restore our joy.

For even though we stand powerless,
Over whatever has to be,
We can be sure that God is in control,
And His voice commands the sea.

IN THE SUFFERING

Look up! "Broken Hearts"

Many eyes are filled with tears, and have suffered broken hearts.
Many lives have ruptured, when all their dreams fell apart.
And at one time or another, we all have felt the pain,
When someone thought carelessly and left us in the rain.

Someone who we loved, suddenly said "goodbye",
And now we feel completely alone, as we question why?
But there are no answers or reasons, for such a cruel betray,
Just an empty feeling, with nothing left to say.

And though our heart still cries out for, the love we thought was true,
We now must try to start over, and find someone that's new.
So let us look up! "Broken hearts", someone is standing by,
For Jesus wants to wipe away, every tear we cry.

He wants to replace our past loves, with His Love so pure,
And heal the hurt and deepened scars, with His Everlasting Cure.
And He will pick up the pieces that have been shattered in our soul,
If we give Him our love, and complete control.

If we let Jesus mend our broken hearts, then no one can destroy,
The special heart, filled with His Love, and His Endless Joy.

When the Vows Have Been Broken

When the vows have been broken and the love is gone...
And the only music playing is a lonely night song...
Where do you go for comfort?

When the world you've lived in begins to change...
And your life is completely rearranged...
Where is your stability?

Fear and sadness is the emotion you feel;
The pain you are going through is so unreal,
How do you find peace?

Rainbows of color for you have turned gray;
As it gets harder for you to face a new day,
Where is your hope?

Bitterness is in your heart, tears in your eyes...
As you wonder what went wrong
And you question... Why?
Who will help you out?

Jesus is the One who can...
He has restored the broken man.

His Love is dependable and won't disappoint you.
He can even give you back the joy you once knew.

But first you must be willing, to lay down at His feet,
Every trial and heartache that makes you reach defeat.

You must let go of all the sadness and depression in your soul,
And realize Jesus is the answer, by giving Him full control.

For He has the power to free this world from its sin,
And He will create in you the will to love again.

IN THE SUFFERING

Panic Attack

It takes me, controls me and holds me in captivity,
There's darkness, no freedom, no peace I feel or see...

I find it in the smallest things, like the news on the TV.
My life can spin around and round until I'm dizzy...

But Lord, you still hold me, you steady me,
In Your Love, I find hope of such serenity.

Doubt may take stolen hours and frightened I may be...
But, you are still in control and hold eternity.

My purpose is sure; my future is secure, my destiny...
Fear is now losing its grip, like calmness in a sea

Now that I have cried out to You, down on bended knee,
I feel Your Peace once more, because You heard my plea.

Troubled Thoughts

When misery loves company, it's easy for me to see,
All of my problems and focus is on me.

But gently I hear the Spirit, whisper to my heart,
Words of wisdom and love He has spoken from the start.

All sadness, disappointment or pain that I feel,
Is entrusted to God and His plan revealed.

Perhaps, not right away or anytime soon,
But one day at a time, my heart is attuned...

For the possibilities are so much more...
If I stop my complaining and whining galore.

My acts of kindness can give Glory to God,
By helping others out, as I travel a sod.

So go away troubled thoughts, I will not share,
Anymore of your time, that captures me there.

I have found a Love, that nothing can separate,
A life worth living, that God will consecrate.

I will give endless praise, unto my Lord,
And my heart will find its greatest reward.

IN THE SUFFERING

Blessing Before Bitterness

My heart has been ripped out,
I understand what pain is about,
Once my depression was at its worse.

What happened to me was unfair,
So I fell into great despair,
Believing that love was just a curse.

For I have been treated so mean and cruel,
When I was obeying all the rules,
And I just couldn't understand...

How someone could be so heartless and bold,
To leave my love out in the cold,
When I had never made any demands.

So harboring bitterness deep inside,
With anger and hate to the Lord I cried,
"I will never forgive them for what they've done".

But Jesus quickly reminded me,
Of what a Christian is supposed to be,
And how we are to live as an example for everyone.

I told Him, "Lord it's hard to accept,
When promises made were not kept,"
But He said, "Show them Love"...

"By giving them blessings like I've given you,
No matter what they put you through,
For this is what pleases your Father above".

Bystander's Prayer

One morning I received a call, while I was still in bed,
Telling of an accident, a fear I often dread.

As I gathered my things together and left in a hurry,
My mind was filled with many thoughts, trying not to worry.

Yet, on the way I felt the prayers, that I needed in that hour,
And through all of the uncertainty, I also felt God's Power.

Have you ever felt the Hand of God, through the Power of Prayer?
Have you ever been all alone, then found somebody cared?

A day when everything was wrong, suddenly felt right,
A time when darkness started closing in, you found the strength to fight.

A time when you were afraid but had the courage to see it through,
These are the moments when someone remembered to pray for you.

These who are faithful, are ready to intercede,
On our behalf, for someone else or for a stranger who is in need.

They pray for the fallen, the restless and confused,
They pray for the homeless, the helpless and abused.

They pray when they are awakened in the dead of the night,
For a soul who has been lost, searching for God's Light.

Prayers from God's servants who have answered many pleas,
By standing on the prayer wall and falling to their knees.

Each time these prayers reach Heaven, our God is Glorified,
By every peaceful, prayerful word, the bystander's prayer has cried.

Oh shall we not be available too, ready to pray as well,
For those we know and know us not, may all our prayers prevail.

The Lighthouse

There is an old house, by the seaside,
That stands so tall, against the tide,
It shows a light, so it may be,
Guidance to the ones at sea.

It never fails to show its light,
To ships that pass by, through the night.
It saved one ship, and many more,
This old house, by the shore.

Well, this brings my story to an end,
But please consider this my friend...
Each one of us are ships at sail,
That need be guided away from hell.

The world is like the tempest sea,
That makes it hard for you and me.
But wait this isn't the end of the line,
We also have a Light which shines.

Jesus is our Light, call on Him and be saved,
Those of you, who are tossed by the waves,
For if He sees, your ship by night,
He will surely, show you the Light.

The Trusting Time

Storms are over me the clouds are so gray,
And yet this is not what casts my fear.
Tis the sunny time when all is at play,
The daily grind that I live each year.

Moments of bliss seem fleeting,
Discouragement takes me unaware,
The enemy gleefully depleting,
The Hand of God's Infinite Care.

Why does my heart who knows Jesus,
Struggle with insecurities beyond measure.
Why must my mind put up such a fuss,
When it holds such an eternal treasure.

Sometimes verses are read and songs are sung,
Yet, the Presence of God is quiet still.
The enemy gloats and has his fun,
But, Lord, this is not THY WILL...

No, this is only the Trusting Time,
Oh that my heart would pass thy test...
And a stronger Faith in you I'd find,
While I abide within Your chest.

Trust in God

To trust in God for our salvation, is that all we trust Him for?
Or does God expect us to trust Him, for a whole lot more.

How can we not trust God, for our daily little strife?
If we once trusted Him... to save our very life,

Is the time not quick enough, according to His Plan?
That makes us want to take matters, into our own hands.

Surely, the Lord who has saved our lowly Hell bound soul,
Can be trusted enough to give Him, complete control.

So many times we've failed Him, and showed no faith at all,
Because we didn't give to Him, our problems very small.

God doesn't weigh our strife,
To see what's too heavy or light,

He just says cast all of our cares upon Him,
And He will make things right.

Just Remember

Days are often filled with uncertain turns and twists,
Some are good and bad, while others merely exist.
We try to make the best of things, to give us strength to cope,
But when tragedy seems to befall us, it takes away our hope.

Being a Christian has its moments, in which we cannot see,
A direct path where God is leading us to a victory.
When clouds of darkness and shadows of despair, try to conceal our joy,
We sometimes will fall into depression, which seeks only to destroy.

But if we look beyond our situations, and just follow in God's Will,
Then our eyes are kept on Jesus, and our spirit He will fill.
And we can take comfort in knowing, that one day we will see,
The Blessed Hope of the Risen Christ, throughout eternity.

IN THE SUFFERING

Point to Him

When we see someone who is broken,
Sometimes it's best, to keep our words unspoken.

If we find someone who is caught in sin,
Let us gently try to restore them again.

If someone is full of great despair,
Let them know how much you care.

If someone is ill or feeling sick,
Encouragement always does the trick.

You see even though we like to give advice and compare,
What people really need is the silence of our prayers.

Whether the person is sad, upset or distressed,
A lot of times it can be the best...

To not instruct or give information,
But rather share God's Word with exhortation.

Being very careful, that we don't control,
Or else we'll miss out on moments, that help console.

Because in every given situation no matter how grim,
God is in control and we should always point to Him.

My Constant

Where can I go, that You are not there?
For my Lord, You are everywhere.
Your hand does guide me and takes me through,
The daily grind of life's issues.

The surprises and joys that I celebrate,
I receive Your blessings, when I do wait,
For Your perfect timing, to be in my life,
Your wisdom does keep me, away from much strife.

You know me and search me in the deepest part,
For You created me from Your very heart.
When I was in my mother's womb,
Even there, Your love bloomed.

Your mind is full of sovereignty,
To understand You, is too much for me.
If I find myself flying, through the sky,
Your Presence is still nearby.

On the ground, when I'm running from fear,
I can be assured that You are here.
When I choose life's hell, by my will,
It is there You are with me, leading me still.

So fill me, consume me and convict my soul,
I want to hold nothing back, from Your control,
Do not let sin break, my fellowship with You,
Restore me and dwell in my spirit anew.

Let the dark not cover me, without seeing a shine,
Of Your Radiant Presence, in my life intertwined.
With Your Glory, Honor and Power to show,
Your Holiness and Majesty in my life overflowed.

Beautiful Lullaby

When I am lonely and broken,
I am comforted by words unspoken.
When I am desolate and have nowhere to go,
There is One who still loves me so.

When I am sinful and full of shame,
There is One who calls me by name.
When I've been betrayed and misled,
There is One who lifts my head.

He calms me with His quiet presence,
Within His arms I find acceptance.
My sleepless nights I find remedy,
In the sound of His endless melody.

As God sings over me throughout the night,
I sleep ever soundly by His touch of moonlight.
In every confidence and through every fear,
He's holding my hand and I can sometimes hear...

The rustle of angels wings when God is near by,
As over me he sings a beautiful lullaby.

If We Will Only Have Faith

So many times we forget about Jesus,
And we let our minds slip away.

Then our eyes will grow dim,
And we cannot see Him.
All because we didn't have faith.

So many times when our lives are so troubled,
And our hearts are filled with despair.

We seldom take time to call on our Lord,
We seem to forget He is there.

We've got to lean on Him,
Trust in His Wisdom,
When things aren't going our way.

Then we will find,
He will show us the answer,
If we will only have faith.

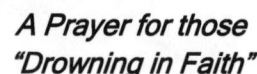

A Prayer for those "Drowning in Faith"

*Heavenly Father, we praise You for
You are Holy and True. We need You now.
We ask that You forgive us where we have
fallen short and where we have doubted You.
Please give us Your Strength, Your Courage
and Your Peace. We are burdened by so many troubles,
trials and struggles. Still, we know You have blessed us
richly and we are thankful. Let us trust YOU more and
trust You to fight our battles as we wait
for the victory. In Jesus Name, Amen.*

From My Heart:

*Life's reality can often be cruel, confusing and calloused.
Yet, when we go through various trials and struggles, sometimes
the truth has the potential of revealing if our identity is one
of its own or one that belongs to Christ.*

From God's Heart:

*God is our refuge and strength, an ever-present help in trouble.
Therefore we will not fear, though the earth give way and the
mountains fall into the heart of the sea, though its waters roar
and foam and the mountains quake with their surging.
(Psalm 46:1-3)*

DROWNING FAITH

IN THE SUFFERING

Going a little farther, he fell with his face to the ground and prayed, "My Father, if it is possible, may this cup be taken from me. Yet not as I will, but as you will." Matthew 26:39

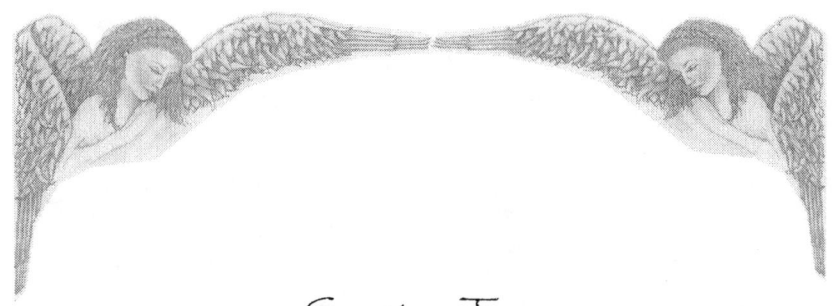

Section Two
Disguised Blessing

Disguised Blessing

I've seen this door many times in my life
When those I've loved have encountered its strife.
Yet, here I am, it's my turn now,
I don't know which way to turn or how.
I must confess, I'm full of fear,
To ever think I would be standing here.
Will I live through this pain and suffering?
Even now it awaits my entering.
My life is no different than any other soul,
Where weakness and sickness have taken its toll.
Yet, in the midst of what I feel...
Beyond the pain or shattered will,
Is the Presence of another who has endured much loss,
Not just pain and suffering but a death on a cross.
Jesus was sacrificed for a life like mine,
I have heard people say countless times.
Many moments in my life I turned Him away,
But now I am compelled to ask Him to stay.
For I need the Hope that He is offering to me,
Not just for physical healing but for an Eternity.
I can feel Him now holding me near,
Assuring my heart that He is here.
So I accept this trial and all that it will bring,
Because I know it has become my disguised blessing.

Faith for Winter

Lonely, depressed and blue, the snow falls to the ground,
Cold, wet, and dreary is the weather all around.

My heart is distilled, longing after more,
Hidden is the Faith I had long before...

Now the winter comes, with her whispering wind,
And I am troubled with trials, in my life again.

So, now I call to You, to rescue me from despair,
Spark my Faith once more and kindle it with care.

Cover me my Lord, against the cold of winter,
And I will lean on You, as Your Presence I do enter.

Safe from all that can harm me, safe from every fear,
I will build my life around You, for You are always near.

IN THE SUFFERING

In God's Hand

A mother sparrow left her nest, hoping she would find,
Some food to feed her baby birds that she'd left behind.
But later when she returned, with her motherly care,
She found her little baby birds, were no longer there.

In fear she flew from tree to tree, in search for her young,
But they were nowhere to be found, and the day was done.
All through the night the mother sparrow, waited in concern,
Hoping that her baby birds would have a safe return.

Then suddenly, she heard a chirp, so she flew down to see,
And there were her baby birds, as safe as could be.
So amazed she began to realize, that they had not been alone,
For she had found, that God knew best, and He took care of His own.

So many times like the mother sparrow, we are torn apart,
When we worry about the ones, who are precious to our heart.
Circumstances that we can't handle tear at our fragile soul,
And we cease to believe, that God is still in control.

So in despair we search to find, the answers out our self,
But by doing this we only set, God upon the shelf.
For He is there to help us out, in our needed hour,
And when we put our faith in Him, we find His Strength and Power.

So we must always trust in Him, and then we will understand,
That God watches over the ones we love, as He holds them in His hand.

Final Touches

A small stone lying in the ground all dusty and old,
Hardly one would recognize this small piece was gold.

For it had been wasting away under God's green earth,
Until a miner took it home, he thought it was of worth.

The miner felt that this would be a way to make his trade,
But before it would sell, a price had to be paid.

So, he threw it in the fire, life's greatest test,
Always knowing in the end, he would have the best.

He later retrieved it from the heat and the burning coal,
To find a beauty so enlightening, that all would behold.

So many times as Christians, we often bear the pain,
Of being thrown into the fire, by the world's domain.

God found us wasting away, just as the stone,
So He rescued us, to keep us for His own.

But before He could save us, a price had to be paid,
That's when God sent His Son, so a way for us was made.

Sometimes God will test us, according to His Will,
He Tests every part of us, to see if our faith is real.

He wants to be our Anchor, through the tough times that we face,
Teaching us to rest in His Strength, His Love and His Grace.

He wants us to always trust in Him, as we walk through life's fire,
So He can safely lift us out, onto mountains that are higher.

Then someday after these trials are over,
His face we shall surely see,

And the final touches of our lives will be revealed,
As God's complete Creativity.

IN THE SUFFERING

The Power of Prayer

Often we've heard the phrase, "All we can do now is pray",
When the misfortunes of life, seem to fall our way.

We seem to say it without knowing its Fullness of Power,
Not having enough hope, to brighten our dark hour.

Oh, we can feel God with us, and we know that He cares,
But we wish we could do more, than just go to Him in prayer.

But let us take a moment, away from our fear,
To see what we are missing, that is so very dear.

Our prayer to God, is a miracle in itself,
And we shouldn't take it lightly, nor set it on a shelf.

We have a direct communication, which shouldn't be ignored,
It gives us access to God, through Jesus Christ our Lord.

And with this special blessing, we can do so much,
As God hears our prayers, many lives can be touched.

Pity Party

When I looked at myself and saw a troubled me...
Trying to escape, from all my reality...
I turned to my friends, who seemed to have it all,
But not caring how I felt, they didn't hear my call.

And so I began to dream, of what could have been,
But by thinking of the past, I was sad once again.
So, I had a pity party, just me, myself and I...
And I celebrated sadness with the tears that I cried.

Heartache was there and loneliness brought pain...
They tried to comfort me, but only caused more rain.
Then suddenly I heard a voice, beyond my silent tears,
That relieved me of my sadness and all my dreadful fears.

It was Jesus, who rescued me from my unhappy hour,
And He gave me inner strength, through His Loving Power.
He said that all my moments of sadness would erase...
If I fixed my eyes and heart upon His precious face.

So just remember friend, the next time you can't cope,
Take your eyes off yourself and see the Blessed Hope.

IN THE SUFFERING

The Unanswered Prayer

When times are bad, we turn to prayer,
In faith that God, will meet us there.

And as we kneel upon bended knee,
Earnestly, God hears our plea.

There are times, we pray with care,
When it seems our hearts, reach despair...

We pray so long, with many tears,
And think our prayers, God does not hear.

But He hears all prayers, despite the size,
And we must always, realize...

That He always, answers every cry,
And He will never, pass us by.

You see He answers prayers, within His time,
And we cannot afford, to leave behind...

Anything that we must share,
That should be taken, to God in prayer.

God answers all prayers, this I know,
Sometimes with a yes, sometimes with a no.

And sometimes the answer He gives is to wait,
But in answering our prayers He is never late.

So, do not think that God does not care,
For there is no such thing as an unanswered prayer.

Just to Say

Seasons pass so very fast,
And it's hard to make a moment last.
But we live the best we can,
Even though we misunderstand.

Life's disappointments and unfair ways,
Can take away the brighter days.
Things are fine until there is change,
Then everything is rearranged...

But life here is temporary and we shouldn't be sad,
A Great Day is coming, when all shall be glad.
So, let in some light and don't be sorrowed,
Our time on earth is only borrowed!

For if we have Jesus in our hearts,
One day from this world we will depart!
We'll leave this body, to which we are bound,
And fly to plains, of higher ground.

So I hope you realize that in all you do,
I care a lot and God does too!

IN THE SUFFERING

Trapped Inside

Many years ago, it seems like yesterday,
You would cook me meals and care for me each day.

But now those days are gone, just a faded memory,
All is most forgotten, times that used to be.

Still, the greatest moment, I treasure most of all,
Is the time you taught me God's Word, when I was very small.

I still can hear you singing, the hymn "How Great Thou Art",
I miss your quiet prayers, that broke your gentle heart.

I bring up happy times, when I was just a kid,
I try hard to remind you of what your mind has hid.

But the more that I try, I see nothing left,
Of the "YOU", I once knew... now trapped inside yourself.

Sometimes I feel lost, disheartened and sad,
When I fail to recover, what we once had.

Your physical health, is as strong as it can be,
But your mind is gone, you no longer recognize me.

I feel at times I need you and don't know what to do,
I miss all the conversations, I used to have with you,

God's Love, His Word and promises are all you ever knew,
And now I too, must hold onto Him, as I muddle through.

I know His Love for me is constant and with me evermore,
Still, you are not here, at least not like before.

Yet, it is God that I cling to, through every trying hour,
Giving me the strength, for He is my Strong Tower.

Because with every visit, every smile, I still can see God's care,
And though you are trapped inside, He holds you safely there.

I'm Still Here

Alone she sits on her bed,
Trying to remember what people have said.
Yet, she can't recall the moment when,
The day has begun or when it will end.

Oh but if you could just imagine with me,
A different person entirely.
One who was wiser and much younger,
Full of strength and vigor.

Someone who could cook and do laundry,
As she took care of her family.
An energetic wife and mother,
Who still made time for helping others.
A different time and yesterday,
When she would laugh at the things you'd say.

When she would pray and sing hymns,
She could brighten any room that was dim.
She loved sharing Jesus with everyone,
Especially with children, who were very young.

But now... someone must show her care,
And even pick out the clothes she wears.
Each visit there seems to be a little less,
As she becomes more lost in her emptiness.

But every now and then, I still can find,
A glimmer of Hope by God's design.
For I can almost see in her face,
His Presence glowing with sweet grace.

And I can hear a voice from her very heart,
Whispering His Love with every part.
It says, "Don't worry, I'm still here,
Safe in His Spirit, where God is near".

IN THE SUFFERING

In the Clearing

The older that I get, the more I understand,
How fragile life is slipping through my hands.

The emotions that I feel, that well up in my soul,
Seem meaningless, for I am not in control.

You created my being, when I was just a thought,
I grew with your wisdom, in which I have been taught.

And now as each year passes, I can see so much,
A pathway is marked for me, with Your gentle loving touch.

As youthfulness leaves my body and lines appear on my face,
I feel Your presence even stronger, though life has left its trace.

When changes begin to happen, and seem to creep up on me,
I cherish the moments of my Faith, with childlike simplicity.

This home on earth is fleeting, oh now I see it true,
I am only in the clearing, until I live with You.

Windows of Light

A room full of darkness, I am hiding here,
Away from life's problems, thinking no one really cares.

The view is dismal and gray, no hope can be seen,
A lonely, cold presence is felt, in everything.

Black curtains are hanging, as dark as can be,
No good thing is present no help do I see.

Shall I open a window, to receive a new view?
Perhaps, the air will be refreshing and the sky sea blue.

Birds may be singing a song for His Joy,
And I recall a time, when no one could destroy...

A day when my heart, was filled with Joy and Peace,
Yet today depression has me captive, with no hope of release.

But my prayers can uplift me with His Strength and His Power,
Regardless, of how I am feeling this hour.

The struggle within may be pulling me back,
But my God will help me in any attack.

So, I will open a window, a window of Light,
And all darkness will be, chased into the night.

He Holds You

You knew reflections from a kinder past,
Where joy and laughter seemed to last.

Yet, now there is only an empty stare,
For the person you once knew, is just not there.

This life that once was full of life,
Now endures much heartache and strife.

A different time and place back then,
So long ago, you don't remember when.

For what was once healthy and full of joy,
Has now all but been destroyed.

Perhaps, by an injury, disease or old age,
This person's life is caught in a cage.

A suffering trap, with no way out,
No longer realizing what life is about.

You try to show love in every way,
While caring for them day by day.

DISGUISED BLESSING

You are grateful for the many memories,
As you think back to what used to be.

There are good days, and there are bad,
But, you remain thankful for the times you have had.

So let me encourage anyone out there,
Who care for others and send up prayers,

Whether in a hospital, hospice or place of care,
You can be assured, that God is there.

Though this challenge is taking its toll,
Please remember He's in control.

So listen for His voice as it speaks to your heart,
Tenderness, Compassion and Hope He will impart.

The strength you need, to get you through each hour,
Rests softly within His Loving Power.

He's Holy and Good, and full of Sweet Love,
He guards you with His angels' above.

And just remember even when, you find your faith is too small,
God will hold onto you, and will not let you fall.

IN THE SUFFERING

Looking Beyond

Today my cross is heavy, in which I daily bear,
But I'm comforted by God's Spirit, which is forever there.

Today my soul is weary, and my footsteps are very weak,
But I know my God is Faithful, and His promises He will keep.

For one day when Christ returns, He shall split the sky,
And His face will be seen by every beholden eye.

Then all will sing His praises, with a joyous song,
With love for our Redeemer, in which we've waited for so long.

It's the troubles and trials we endure, that often bring us defeat,
But these crosses will one day be exchanged for crowns,
So we can lay them at Jesus feet.

DISGUISED BLESSING

Waiting on Healing

Are you growing fearful every hour?
Do you need God's Holy Power?
He can help you carry on...

As your eyes well up with tears,
Do you wonder if God hears?
The prayers you've been praying until dawn.

Questions without answers,
Can trip up the joyous dancer,
When no sign is given.

You see sometimes the road is rough,
When our circumstances get tough,
But there can be healing... even if it is in Heaven.

Your strength and faith may have dampened,
By what has yet to have happened.
But God can give you His Peace in your heart.

He can calm the storms in your life,
Or calm YOU during struggles and strife.
Even when your world has fallen apart.

And it's in that moment when,
You are reminded once again,
God Loves you so!

For our prayers are softly held,
In the Hands that have not failed,
And those same Hands will not let you go.

God sees each sparrow that falls,
He hears each child when they call,
And He can give you strength for each day.

He has not abandoned you,
He will help you see this through,
The answers are in the waiting, while you pray.

Eden's Hope

Your trials may be bearing down hard on you,
You may have sickness, you're struggling through...

Or perhaps your grief is too much for you to carry,
Whatever the case, you are tired and weary.

You don't understand where God could be,
And why such moments in life bring misery...

Oh but please listen, my broken-hearted friend,
God is not far, and devastation He does not send.

It all started long ago, when God spoke into place,
Creation's beautiful existence, filling every space.

He placed male and female, in a garden fair,
Everything was perfect as they walked with Him there.

But because of temptation and disobedience,
Death was the disease of Sin's consequence.

For every part of this earth that stretches from land to sea,
Has been affected by sin's fall, even you and me.

DISGUISED BLESSING

Since then many generations have been lost in wanderings,
Through much failure, rebellion and false God offerings...

Yet, a Holy plan was put into place which offered Hope again,
Through the sacrifice of God's own son, so we could live with Him.

As Creation itself cries out for that certain Day,
Those who love Jesus, will watch, wait and pray.

This too is Eden's hope, to be renewed and healed,
A paradise of perfection that one day will be revealed.

So hear this message loudly and hear it very clear,
God Loves You very much and He is always near.

Every living thing has purpose, under God's Heaven above,
From those that we care about to the family pets we love.

Our pain, sickness and grief is all for God to show,
His Son glorified in our lives here below.

So do not lose heart or think that life is meaningless,
Because God is still in control and He is Timeless.

IN THE SUFFERING

I'm Not Afraid to Die

On a road that led to trouble,
On the seas when the waves were to high...

I have been on those roads and oceans,
but I wasn't afraid to die.

I am saved and I'm going to heaven,
And I can't wait to get in that sky...

And when my Christ Jesus calls me,
I won't be afraid to die.

Because He knows, and He watches,
And He sees every tear,
If I'm to die, I have nothing to fear.

He will take me on to live... in that bright sky,
Oh, I'm not afraid to die.

Tell me friend have you met the Savior,
Who can take care of your life...

Ask Him now to come in and save you,
Oh, are you afraid to die?

DISGUISED BLESSING

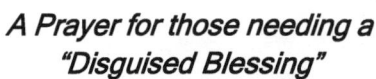

A Prayer for those needing a "Disguised Blessing"

*Heavenly Father, we praise You for
You are Loving and Kind. We need You now.
We ask that You forgive us when we
complain or lash out against You or others.
Please give us Your Strength, Your Courage
and Your Peace. We are burdened by so
much pain, with illness and we are weak.
Still, we know that You have
the Power to heal us if it is in Your Will.
So, we are thankful for the good days
that we have and the less painful ones.
Please help us to trust You more as we await
Your healing not only in our body but in our soul.
May You be Glorified in us. In Jesus Name, Amen.*

From My Heart:

Our physical healing doesn't always happen
but God's Spiritual Healing will never abandon
anyone who seeks Him.

From God's Heart:

*In the same way, the Spirit helps us in our weakness.
We do not know what we ought to pray for, but the Spirit
himself intercedes for us with groans that words cannot express.
And he who searches our hearts knows the mind of the Spirit,
because the Spirit intercedes for the saints in accordance with God's
will. And we know that in all things God works for the good of
those who love him, who have been called according
to his purpose. Romans 8:26-28*

IN THE SUFFERING

It was now about the sixth hour, and darkness came over the whole land until the ninth hour, for the sun stopped shining. And the curtain of the temple was torn in two. Jesus called out with a loud voice, "Father, into your hands I commit my spirit." When he had said this, he breathed his last. Luke 23:44-46

IN THE SUFFERING

Section Three
Dark Hours

IN THE SUFFERING

Dark Hours

You've pulled down the shades, still there can't be,
A darker place for misery,
Than your heart...

What once was alive and filled with joy,
Now grief has all but destroyed,
And torn your world apart...

There you sit in a darkened room,
Full of emptiness and terrible gloom,
Alone in great despair...

There are no words to say,
You have no strength left to pray,
You ask, is there anyone who cares?

Tho answer is yes, my dearest friend,
You need not feel that this is the end,
A Savior is waiting patiently...

He knows the pain and anguish real,
He understands just how you feel,
He suffered on a cross for you and me...

Heaven watched and waited,
As a crowd anticipated,
A crucifixion for all to see...

DARK HOURS

Senseless mocking and torture,
Became a spectacle of disorder,
But the only way to set men free...

Angels stared down from Heaven,
With not a sign given,
To rush in and rescue the One...

So Jesus took His last breath,
Before a very slow death,
He said, "It is Finished, it is Done"...

And for three days, time stood still,
Oh who would think this, to be God's Will?
So death celebrated and danced...

Evil had succeeded, good had failed,
All that was Holy, had been nailed,
To a cruel cross of circumstance.

Until...

The Father gave Life once more,
To His Son who burst through the door,
Into Life Everlasting!

And now this same Hope can be ours,
Even in life's dark hours,
Because of our Risen King!

You may not feel it now,
But grief's fog will lift somehow,
With a lot of time and much prayer...

One day you will too,
Know the joy that you once knew,
But for now, may Jesus hold you in His Care.

IN THE SUFFERING

Before I Miss Today

The doctor has given his diagnosis... the news isn't good,
It's time to start thinking... about the things I should.
Like provisions for my family... when I'm no longer here,
I've taken so much for granted... that I hold so dear.

It's hard to think about... the things that I will miss,
For there are many reminders of living... life in such bliss...
Like hot coffee in the morning... or watching the TV,
Sunrises, sunsets and thunderstorms to see.

Conversations with those that I love... of things I need to say,
I cannot wait, I must tell them now... before I miss today.
And something I've been feeling... but didn't understand,
A truth that I now must face... like every other man.

Compelling me to travel down a road... I've only heard about,
One of supernatural means... I now must settle any doubt.
Concerning a Loving God, forgiveness of sin... and life eternally...
Heaven's gate, loved ones to meet... a Saviors face to see?

Or dare I think, a lonely fate... of past regrets will be...
A Hell's fury, strangers in torment in endless agony.
These questions I must ask myself... while I still have today,
To which place will my soul depart... and softly slip away?

But wait!

This very moment... my heart does hear a Voice,
Shall I ignore this Holy Plea? For I will die with my choice.
Perhaps God will help me now... if only I will pray,
And ask Jesus into my heart... before I miss today.

I Cannot Feel

I cannot feel the emptiness and pain,
Of what you're feeling today,
And I do not have the power or strength,
To remove your thoughts of dismay.

I cannot unfold the hope of tomorrow,
That I know you will find again,
I can only offer you my deepest sympathy,
As one of your many friends.

But my Savior who is standing by,
With all His Loving Grace,
Can offer you the Peace you need,
For whatever you may face.

For He can restore your wounded soul,
And mend your broken heart,
With all His consolation,
That will make your sorrow depart.

As a Friend He will bear your burdens,
And all, your heartaches share,
Still... I will keep you in my thoughts,
And in my every prayer.

IN THE SUFFERING

A Valentine of Praise

Once I held hands with my love so true,
While walking in a park and sitting in a pew.
But now I lift my hands to You,
Use me Lord in all I do.

Once I spoke with romantic gestures,
To my mate and sweetest treasure.
But now I will offer in highest measure,
My voice in praise to bring You pleasure.

Yet, when many memories in my mind repeat,
My life sometimes seems incomplete...
But with my tears so bittersweet,
Let me anoint Thy precious feet.

For though my mate has passed away,
And others know not what to say,
With prayers of hope I humbly pray,
So help me live for You each day.

DARK HOURS

Shadows

After Jesus had walked many days on the earth,
The day had finally arrived... the moment
He would die, to save so many lives.

I saw in the shadows on the ground,
All my darkened sin... Now, they were upon my Lord
In a place where I should have been.

And as the sun disappeared as if it were the night,
I saw shadows once again fall across the sky...

In anguish and shame of what was revealed to me,
I prayed for my forgiveness and God did set me free.

And it was then I realized,
Just how great the cost,

For then I saw... only one shadow left...
The Shadow of the Cross.

The Crucifixion

There once was a man who was arrested,
But no wrong did He do.
He was tried and found innocent,
But He still died for you.
The cruel roman soldiers,
Placed a crown of thorns on His head,
"Every king needs a crown",
Is what the soldiers said.

Then they gave Him a cross to carry,
For it was part of the deal,
And they put a robe upon Him,
And led Him to the hill.
They nailed Him to the cross,
Just to watch Him bleed,
They mocked Him, they pierced His side,
And smote Him with a reed.

He could have called ten thousand angels,
To come down from the sky,
But He stayed upon the cross,
For you He chose to die.
Then about the sixth to the ninth hour,
There was no sun,
And He cried with a loud voice,
"Father! It is Done."

They laid Him in a tomb and thought it was the end,
But He arose from the grave, and started living again.
He's living up in heaven somewhere in the blue,
He died and went through all of this, because He loves you.

Words Cannot Express

Words cannot express,
The pain and unhappiness,
That you are feeling today.

For the loss of your loved one,
Has left you feeling numb,
And no one really knows what to say.

But in each miserable hour,
We can find Strength and Power,
Through Jesus Christ our King.

For He guides our destination,
He knows every frustration,
And He can soften our suffering.

I know the heartache that you feel,
Seems to you, to be unreal,
And you keep asking... Why?

But Christ is holding out His hand,
And He will surely help you stand,
If on His shoulder, you would like to cry.

And though it seems, you're on your own,
You do not have to be alone,
Jesus will help you through it all.

When others cannot help you out,
He will lift all of your doubts,
If on His name, you will only call.

Grief (The Mysterious Gift)

When God made people like you and me,
He gave us vision for our eyes to see,
He gave us sound for our ears to hear,
He gave us love for our hearts to bear.

He gave us thought for our minds to know,
He gave us meaning for our lives to grow.
Yet, in the times when our soul feels despair,
From losing a loved one taken out of our care.

It's then we often ask God... Why?
With bitter tears He hears our cry.
You see He has given us special attention,
To the pain we feel that we don't often mention.
The doubts, the anger... He understands,
All is held in His Loving Hand.

He gives us tears to clear our eyes...
Beyond the storms we see blue skies.
He gives us encouragement to hear the words,
Like Hope and Strength in the songs of birds.
He gives us time to deal with strife,
The Touch of His Grace guards our life.

These gifts from God help me and you.
During moments of grief, He will carry us through.

The Folded Flag

You wore your uniform with Honor, your medals with dignity,
You fought for America's freedom, you protected her Liberty.

You sent many letters back home to us,
While encouraging your brothers in war,

You carried out every command you were given,
As you gave back to others, even more.

I don't have any answers now, while we are standing here,
Staring at this folded flag, through heavy eyes of tears.

But I know that God watched over you, and He heard every prayer,
Even though the gunfire and bombs, created a smoke filled air...

Perhaps, it happened in an instant, with little pain at all,
Or maybe you struggled for a while, as past memories you did recall.

But in that stolen moment... where life flashed before your eyes,
I know you felt God's Hand, reach down from the skies.

You had all the courage of a soldier, your bible at your chest,
And with Jesus as your Savior, you died in peaceful rest.

So, now may we gain Wisdom, from God above on High,
To grant us all His Mercy, as so many have had to die.

Oh let us always remember these, with their stories as we brag,
In loving memory as we treasure...

Our Freedom's Folded Flag.

IN THE SUFFERING

When Bad Things Happen

When bad things happen, what do you do?
Are you fearful, angry or have attitude?
This life brings us change,
There are no guarantees...
For our health, jobs or families.

Trials are meant to grow us,
Bring us closer to God's design...
He is our Sanctifier
As we are being refined.
When you feel frightened,
Does your fear increase?
Let God calm you for He is our Peace.

When you have no money,
And the bills are piling high...
Remember, the Lord is our Provider,
Your needs He will supply.

If you've been trampled down,
Caught in a sinners lure...
Jesus is our Righteousness,
He can make your life pure.

If you have wandered away,
And can't find your way back home,
Jesus is the Shepherd,
Who seeks you as you roam.
If you are sick,
Your body is tired and frail,
Pray to God our Healer,
That He will make you well.

If you find yourself abandoned,
You are now on your own,
Call unto the One who is God alone.

When bad things happen,
The future cannot foretell,
But God is always with us, our Immanuel.

So do not despair or give up hope,
Whatever circumstance should befall,
Just Praise Him, our Adonai, Jesus Lord of all.

DARK HOURS

Angels' Wings

Your heart is so heavy, everything seems surreal,
Through swollen-filled eyes, you cease to feel...
Any joy, contentment or short-lived happiness,
Seems out of your reach, from endless emptiness.

Friends and loved ones try to offer their care,
But grief has paralyzed you so, it's as if no one is there.
I'm sure as you watch this moment unfold,
You long to escape its terrible hold.

Yet, God is also watching, with His angels nearby,
He hasn't missed seeing one tear that you've cried.
His heart is breaking for you, with Compassionate Love.
So, do not think Him distant, or too high above.

Call on Him now in your moment of grief,
He can bring you Peace and sweet relief.
Just listen closely, in your darkest of night,
And you will hear angels' wings, hovering in flight.

Angels are Here

Angels are here,
They hover, they are silent,
Yet they are very near.
Quietly in the midst,
They listen to every prayer.

Through the dark shadows,
On the brightest day,
They watch they linger...
And hear us when we pray.

Protecting us, surrounding us
They are angels unaware,
They are invisible reminders,
That God still cares.

In times of weeping,
In times of joy,
There constant presence...
Evil can't destroy.

God's angels of light,
Showing us His way,
Standing right beside us,
As they guard us this day.

DARK HOURS

Why Do Bad Things Happen

What words can someone say...
That will take the pain away?

What comfort can be shown...
That will erase the fears unknown?

For when bad things change our lives,
We all must question... Why?

And as circumstances rip into our soul...
Why can't we gain control?

Why do bad things happen? ...
It's a question of the heart,

And there is no easy answer,
to keep us from falling apart.

But the suffering can be consoled,
If in Christ we do believe,

And He will wipe away the tears,
And our pain relieve...

For though we all must suffer,
We suffer not alone,

And we will find the Hope in knowing,
God is still on His Throne.

IN THE SUFFERING

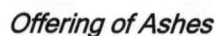

Offering of Ashes

As you sit and stare,
Your heart no longer cares,
For what happens to you.

At one time your heart sang,
But now all that remains,
Is a sad song, with a lonely tune.

Bitterness, hurt and anger,
Have placed you in danger,
Of ever coming out of your shell.

Expectations have been dashed,
All your dreams have crashed,
As grief wears its face so well.

All the prayers that you pleaded,
They were not interceded,
And you feel betrayed.

God chose an ultimate healing,
Which has left you reeling,
And your faith is tattered and frayed.

DARK HOURS

Your appearance is disheveled,
Because your life has been leveled,
And normal will never be right.

The death of your loved one,
Has left you feeling numb,
And you haven't the strength to fight.

Let Jesus fight this battle,
For He alone can handle,
Every broken piece of your heart.

He can chase away the darkness,
And expel that which seems hopeless,
By giving you a fresh new start.

So give to him your fears,
Your pain and falling tears,
And everything that brings you dismay.

For He can restore each day that passes,
With your offering of ashes,
And turn it into Joy again one day.

IN THE SUFFERING

Trembling Hope

You think I'd learn,
You would think I would know,

How this would end...
How this would go...

For I know God watches over me,
And He controls my destiny.

Still fear would try to undo,
All that faith has seen me through.

But when you're looking at an unknown door,
It becomes difficult to pray... anymore.

Yet when I cry out in desperation,
My Lord can help my situation.

So, I will now let go of my last rope,
And trust Him with my trembling hope.

My Savior Walks By Me

I can hear the Footsteps follow,
As I'm walking down my way...

I can see the Hand that guides me,
Through my troubles every day...

And I know that it's my Savior,
Whose Love is protecting me...

He waits for me in Heaven,
Where someday I know I'll be.

I can hear the wind that's blowing,
Outside where there's a storm...

But I just keep on knowing,
To me there'll come no harm...

For He walks by me so closely,
And I know that He is there...

And it makes my life worth living,
Just to know my Savior cares.

And He sits on the right hand of the Father,
Looking down from the sky that I see...

And until I go and meet Him,
I know my Savior always walks by me.

A Prayer for those who are in the "Dark Hours"

Heavenly Father, we praise You for Your Comfort and Compassion. We need You now. We ask that You forgive us in the moments when we have thought You to be distant, un-caring or unkind. Please give us Your Strength, Your Comfort and Your Peace. We are so burdened by grief, despair and deepest sorrow. We feel like our hearts have been crushed and ripped out of our chest. Still, we are thankful for the life of those that we grieve for and for the memories that we have of them. Please help us to trust You as You Restore, Renew and Restart our lives again. Help us to take one day at a time but with each day let us see Your Hope and then someday maybe even have Joy again. In Jesus Name, Amen.

From My Heart:

Grief can make us feel and think God is far away but be encouraged because He has taken a front row seat where we are. Even if that is when we are kneeling beside a hospital bed or at the graveside of a loved one.

From God's Heart:

So I say, "My splendor is gone and all that I had hoped from the LORD." I remember my affliction and my wandering, the bitterness and the gall. I will remember them, and my soul is downcast within me. Yet this I call to mind and therefore I have hope: Because of the LORD's great love we are not consumed, for his compassions never fail. They are new every morning; great is your faithfulness. I say to myself, "The LORD is my portion; therefore I will wait for him."
Lamentations 3:18-24

DARK HOURS

IN THE SUFFERING

The angel said to the women, "Do not be afraid, for I know that you are looking for Jesus, who was crucified. He is not here; he has risen, just as he said..." Matthew 28:5-6

Section Four
Divine Hope

IN THE SUFFERING

Divine Hope

After the blood fell and dripped to the ground,
Beyond the screams and many sounds,
A Father waited...

Heavy hearts dealt with gore,
Of removing hands and feet that tore,
As hope faded...

Heaven watched intently as the Son now rested,
Disciples ran and hid as their faith was sorely tested,
Hearts began to cry aloud...

Loved ones took such gentle care,
For the lifeless body, laying there,
And wrapped it in a shroud...

It was placed in a tomb so cold,
Then soldiers stood and guarded bold,
The dead Nazarene...

One day went by and then another,
What seemed a nightmare to all the others,
Was mankind's opening...

Then suddenly in the dark of night,
Or maybe at early morning's light,
Something started to happen...

An earthquake shook with great thunder,
A stone rolled away in surrender,
For Life's new beginning...

For inside, the body that laid still,
Which had been put there by Sovereign Will,
Started to stir...

Strength returned to the nail scarred hands,
Breath overcame death's demands,
As a miracle occurred.

DIVINE HOPE

Light shattered the dark and gloom,
Of this tiny carved out tomb,
As linen was folded in place.

Heaven rejoiced with sweetest song,
As the day broke with early dawn,
And Jesus now lifted His face.

Though chaos still rules in Hell's domain,
Everyone can now proclaim,
Jesus is risen and is alive!

For all that death tried to capture,
Love has set free in Glorious rapture,
And the world's Hope has finally arrived.

Our story is told through this Hope,
While we wait and try to cope,
Each day we deal with what life brings...

But the message of the Resurrection,
Will bring Renewal and Perfection,
To all who wait for our King!

One day we'll see a great tomorrow,
Where we will never again know sorrow,
And tears will be wiped from our eyes...

Our loved ones we shall meet,
As we sit at our Savior's feet,
This will be our Divine Hope realized.

IN THE SUFFERING

A Hope for Spring

Many nights I have felt an icy pain of despair,
The sun's daylight hid within the frosty air.
Yet now I feel the joy unfolding,
As winter loses the grip it was holding.

Safely it arrives once more,
Spring enters through winter's door.
And I see the sun peering through,
As if to say, "God still loves you".

It touches leaves upon the trees,
The flowers bloom in delicacy.
Reminders of God's Loving Care,
Erase life's winter that was hard to bear.

Soon, even troubles will pass,
They cannot stand they will not last.
For the cold and gloom must depart,
As now the Hope of Spring grows in my heart.

DIVINE HOPE

Even the Flowers Knew

One day many years ago, clouds filled the sky,
Darkness hovered over all the earth, when Jesus was crucified.
Birds that sang such pretty songs, could not sing out a tune,
For even the beautiful flowers knew and so they did not bloom.

Rushing waters that filled the streams, suddenly were still,
Grass began to wither, upon the greenest hills,
Life itself had become extinct and began to fade,
For the Joy and Peace of God was buried where Jesus laid.

But though it seemed Love was lost and all Hope was gone,
The sun started breaking through, to bring a brand new dawn.
For Jesus Christ had risen and elation filled the air,
The trees rejoiced with gladness and peace was everywhere.

For the birds were restored their singing, life was fresh as spring,
The hills exclaimed the victory, to every living thing.
The flowers sprang out in every color, filling every space,
For life had been touched by the Hands of God, by His Wonderful Grace.

And the miracle reached to every stream and every oceans shore,
For Jesus Christ is yesterday, today and forevermore.

Victorious Over All

One day I'll join an army, where I will take a stand,
Along with other Christians, for our Lord's command.

Together we will fight, for Truth and Inner Peace,
And Vengeance will be God's, when His wrath shall be released.

We will be fighting against evil, and God's Love will prevail,
When Satan and his angels, are cast into Hell.

Then the Victory will be the Lord's, as we shout and sing,
Praise be to our God, and our Heavenly King.

But until then we fight a battle, in our lives every day,
Against the powers of darkness, that try to stand in our way.

Yet, God gives us courage, so we can fight back.
Through trials and temptations, that can get us off track,

And with the Sword of Truth, to guide us, we will remain strong,
We can defeat the enemy, and all that is wrong.

We may not win every battle, sometimes we will fall,
But we will keep Hope in knowing, God is VICTORIOUS OVER ALL.

My Prayer of Praise

Dear Lord, this prayer is just for You,
Though my small words, will never do.
For they cannot begin to show,
The greatest things, I've come to know.

And these words cannot say,
All that is on my heart today.
In times of my life, I can look back and see,
How very close, You walked with me.

And when I would trust You, with all my fears,
You were there, through all those years.
And now my faith in You has grown,
No greater Love, I've ever known.

So, in Your name, this honor be given,
The Highest Praise, throughout the heavens.
For You are Worthy, my Lord Most High,
For my sins, You chose to die.

But in the tomb, one could not hold,
Such power and love that would unfold.
And my life to You I gave,
So my soul, You would save.

So if anything, I ever do,
Does not give the Glory to You,
Let me count it all loss and strive to gain,
The things for You that will remain.

Taking a Moment

In life's busy moments, we all must slip away,
And think of a more perfect place, that we shall see one day.

At times when we are stuck in traffic, we need to interrupt,
This moment of confusion, by lifting our eyes up.

For all the problems of this world, that makes up our daily grind,
Need a break with thoughts from Heaven, to give us peace of mind.

Because one day we will all be home, and Jesus will be there,
And it's time to get excited, for that day is drawing near.

So let us take a moment, away from this world's cruelty,
And concentrate on Heaven, where we'll spend eternity.

The Great Ecstasy

As I watch the clouds, swiftly pass in the sky,
I hear songs from the birds, as over me they fly.
While enjoying this moment, I begin to slip away,
Releasing my problems, and all I've been through today.

I imagine the rapture, where in the air I will rise,
To meet my Coming King, and Lord Most High.
For I can't wait until, He scatters the night,
Filling every corner, of this earth, with His Light.

Such majesty my eyes, will one day behold,
His coming will be GREAT, as prophets have foretold.
Because I will see Jesus, in all His Glory as He is,
And all Praise and Honor will forever be His.

And I look forward in hearing, His Words so sweet,
"Well done my faithful servant, Come sit at my feet".

The Main Attraction

When I get to Heaven, it will be so nice,
To enter the pearly gates, which are worth great price.

And when I walk on streets of gold, how lovely they will be,
But even this will not compare, to Heaven's specialty.

For Heaven's main attraction, will still be at hand,
When I join with all the others, and I proudly stand.

To sing praises to our King, with the angel's choir,
For this is what I long for, and I most desire.

It will be fine to see the River of Life,
And Tree of Knowledge, standing tall,

But when I lay my eyes on Jesus,
That will be the greatest sight of all.

For a place like Heaven would not exist, if Jesus wasn't there,
With His Light Shining Radiance, or His Beauty fair.

And even if His home was not Heaven, it would not matter to me,
For Jesus is the only part of Heaven, I truly want to see.

Heaven Presents "Jesus"

Ladies and Gentlemen, you are about to behold,
Life's greatest event, to ever unfold.

For behold you now, is about to take place,
A moment that shall be filled, with Glory and Grace.

So now, without further ado, let us all sing,
As Heaven presents "JESUS", our King.

And here He is now, forever He shall reign,
Oh worthy is the Lamb, for sinners He was slain.

But now He's come to rule, in Majesty and Power,
See Him now in His Glory, as we worship Him this hour.

Such Light and Radiance, beams from His head,
As He establishes to everyone, that He is not dead!

The view of Him is astounding, as He approaches the crowd,
Heavenly Host are singing, and Praising Him aloud.

They sing "Hosanna to our King", as they fall to their knees,
For He comes to bring us Joy, and Everlasting Peace.

And now all eyes are upon Him, as He begins to speak,
"My Children the battle is over, now you shall live with Me".

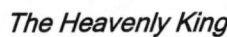

The Heavenly King

What kind of King would come down to earth,
And in a manger lay?

The KING who will bring great things,
Yet many turn Him away.

What kind of King would reject all of earth's
Money, fame and power?

The KING who healed the lepers,
In their needed hour.

What kind of King would ride in town,
On a donkey of disgrace?

The KING who wipes away the tears,
Off every crying face.

What kind of King would in service,
Wash His disciples feet?

The KING that let roman soldiers,
His back badly beat.

What kind of King that being innocent,
Would on a cross die?

The KING who suffered death,
For sinners such as I.

What kind of King would be buried in a tomb,
He borrowed from a friend?
The KING that arose from the grave,
And is now living again.

What kind of King will one day return,
And all shall cry out His name?
JESUS CHRIST the HEAVENLY KING,
FOREVER HE SHALL REIGN.

Poured Out

Tears of brokenness and strength,
Poured right out of me,
Your Truth to hear aloud,
It did my heart so proud.

Yet, the thought of just one soul,
Not knowing the death toll,
Made my heart just break,
And my body did shake.

Father, I must not hesitate,
Before it is too late,
Burden my heart to tell,
So others won't go to Hell.

Honest Worship

God, I want to worship You more!
I want my tears, my heart...
To pour out worship for only YOU!

For You are my Christ, You are my King,
My Savior who gives my heart, a reason to sing,
Creator, over every living thing!

My honest worship and sacrifice do I bring.
Underneath Your Guiding Wings,
Let nothing far or in between,
Ever stop me from entering...

Into Your Holy Presence.

Prepare Me for Eternity

Though I've never seen Your face,
I've felt Your Saving Grace.

I worship You day by day,
Trying to follow in Your Way.

But sometimes I wonder,
And my heart often ponders,
If I really know, who You are to me...

For Thou Art Holy and so great,
And You know my destined fate.

Though You are a King of Power,
You watch over me every hour.

As You live in Heaven above,
Reaching out to me with Love,
I'm surrounded by You, in all I see...

But Lord I want to know You more,
For Thou Art the One I adore.

So fill my human empty soul,
And in my life take full control.

Not leaving one part for my gain,
But always confirming that You shall reign,
As You prepare me for Eternity.

Joy is in the Journey

Even though this world is sometimes hard to bear,
And others have tried to comfort me...

I know my hope is in Christ Loving Care,
And one day His face I will see.

Now you might not quite understand,
Just the way the Lord makes me feel...

But He gives me a Peace so deep inside,
And I know that He is real.

If you would like to share this traveling with me,
Then come follow by His side...

For He will walk with you all the way,
And in His love you will surely find

As we live each day of life,
Although it is filled with pain...

I know it will one day be worth it all,
And we will have all to gain,

Because the Joy is in the Journey,
And the future looks so bright,

Yes, it makes the traveling easier,
When we can see His Light.

DIVINE HOPE

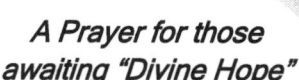

A Prayer for those awaiting "Divine Hope"

*Heavenly Father, we praise You for
You are our God of Eternal Joy and Hope!
We need you now. We ask that You forgive us when
we lose sight of this and take our eyes off Jesus. Please
give us a Renewed Hope as we watch, wait and pray for
Christ's Return! We are burdened by the temporal trials,
sickness and sorrow in our lives that overwhelm us with what
seems to appear as hopeless situations. Still, we are so thankful
that our Hope is in You and in Your Son Jesus! We rejoice in
His Resurrection! Please help us to remember that You are
preparing a place for Your people to live with You for Eternity.
May we always be ready to shine Your Hope within our hearts
so that others can know Jesus! In Jesus Name, Amen.*

From My Heart:

To have hope is more than to make a wish or cross our fingers for a positive result. It is when our prayers of Faith in Jesus meet up with God's Power from Heaven. This Hope once brought back Life to Jesus' lifeless body in a tomb. This Hope will offer the same kind of Resurrection when Believers encounter a physical death, where they will enter into an Eternity to meet our Loving Risen Savior!

From God's Heart:

*Praise be to the God and Father of our Lord Jesus Christ!
In his great mercy he has given us new birth into a living hope through
the resurrection of Jesus Christ from the dead, and into an inheritance
that can never perish, spoil or fade--kept in heaven for you, who
through faith are shielded by God's power until the coming of the
salvation that is ready to be revealed in the last time. In this you
greatly rejoice, though now for a little while you may have had
to suffer grief in all kinds of trials.   I Peter 1:3-6*

IN THE SUFFERING

An Invitation for You

Sinner's Prayer

Oh Lord, I know I am a sinner, this I realize,
And I've heard that You forgive all sins, despite the size.

So I'm asking Your forgiveness, for everything I've done,
And I want You to be my Savior, now while I'm still young.

And now after living in sin, not knowing what to do,
I'm ready to leave the world behind, and follow after You.

So now please come into my heart, and rescue me from sin,
And let me be of service to You, and know You more... Amen.

From My Heart:

If you have not placed your faith in Jesus and accepted Him as your Savior, you can do so right now. Jesus is waiting to come into your life and save you. It doesn't matter what you have or haven't done. It doesn't matter where you are or even how much time you have let slip by you. If you are reading this now it isn't too late and God is presenting this Divine Appointment just for you.

From God's Heart:

*For all have sinned and fall short of
the glory of God. Romans 3:23*

*For God so loved the world that he gave his one
and only Son, that whoever believes in him shall
not perish but have eternal life. John 3:16*

*For the wages of sin is death, but the gift of God is
eternal life in Christ Jesus our Lord. Romans 6:23*

*For it is by grace you have been saved, through
faith--and this is not from yourselves, it is the gift of
God-- not by works, so that no one
can boast. Ephesians 2:8-9*

IN THE SUFFERING

Personal Reflections for
Your Own Journey

Troubles, trials and struggles come,
But for us there is One,
Who can strengthen the undone,
To Jesus, Jesus—shall we run.

PERSONAL REFLECTIONS

Reflections from Section One, Drowning Faith

In what way has God encouraged you personally through section one, "Drowning Faith"?

_____
_____
_____
_____
_____
_____
_____
_____
_____
_____
_____
_____
_____
_____
_____
_____
_____
_____
_____
_____
_____
_____
_____

What troubles, trials or struggles are you presently "drowning in" where you need Jesus to rescue you?

PERSONAL REFLECTIONS

Write out a list of all the things that are heavy on your heart. Next, one by one, begin to send up a prayer to God asking Him to show you how to walk on water with Him.

IN THE SUFFERING

What encouragement of your own can you offer to someone else about what God has taught you concerning your journey of faith?

_____
_____
_____
_____
_____
_____
_____
_____
_____
_____
_____
_____
_____
_____
_____
_____
_____
_____
_____
_____
_____
_____
_____
_____

Personal Notes

Sickness, pain and disease,
Will often bring us to our knees,
But there is One who hears our pleas,
Jesus, Jesus is our Peace.

Reflections from Section Two, Disguised Blessing

In what way has God encouraged you personally through section two, "Disguised Blessing"?

_____
_____
_____
_____
_____
_____
_____
_____
_____
_____
_____
_____
_____
_____
_____
_____
_____
_____
_____
_____
_____
_____
_____
_____

In what way are you suffering Physically? Emotionally? Spiritually?

PERSONAL REFLECTIONS

Write out a list of all the ways that God has blessed you during any past or present suffering. Next, one by one, send up a prayer of Thanksgiving for His Goodness.

What encouragement of your own can you offer to someone else about what God has taught you concerning your journey of suffering?

PERSONAL REFLECTIONS

Personal Notes

Grief, emptiness and gloom,
May have us captured in a room,
But Hope has found its bloom,
Jesus, Jesus rose from the tomb!

PERSONAL REFLECTIONS

Reflections from Section Three, Dark Hours

In what way has God encouraged you personally through section three, "Dark Hours"?

_____
_____
_____
_____
_____
_____
_____
_____
_____
_____
_____
_____
_____
_____
_____
_____
_____
_____
_____
_____
_____
_____
_____

In what areas of your life do you feel hopeless?

PERSONAL REFLECTIONS

Write a list of all the ways grief has paralyzed who you are. Next, one by one, send up a prayer for God to turn your ashes of mourning into His Joy and Hope!

What encouragement of your own can you offer to someone else about what God has taught you concerning your journey of grief?

_____
_____
_____
_____
_____
_____
_____
_____
_____
_____
_____
_____
_____
_____
_____
_____
_____
_____
_____
_____
_____
_____
_____

PERSONAL REFLECTIONS

Personal Notes

The Joy we have shall one day be,
When from this life we are set free,
To live with Christ Eternally,
Oh Jesus, Jesus—shall we see!

PERSONAL REFLECTIONS

Reflections from Section Four, Divine Hope

In what way has God encouraged you personally through section four, "Divine Hope"?

How has Jesus' Resurrection brought Hope to your life (past, present and future)?

PERSONAL REFLECTIONS

Write a list of all the things that you imagine Heaven to be like and that you look forward to seeing one day. Next, one by one, send up a prayer for God to remind you to focus on what is Eternal rather than what is Temporal.

_____
_____
_____
_____
_____
_____
_____
_____
_____
_____
_____
_____
_____
_____
_____
_____
_____
_____
_____
_____
_____
_____
_____
_____
_____

What encouragement of your own can you offer to someone else about what God has taught you concerning your journey of Hope?

_____
_____
_____
_____
_____
_____
_____
_____
_____
_____
_____
_____
_____
_____
_____
_____
_____
_____
_____
_____

Personal Notes

Personal Notes

Verses to Cling to

Verses to Cling to:

My soul clings to you; your right hand upholds me. Psalm 63:8

Clinging to His Strength:

But those who hope in the LORD will renew their strength. They will soar on wings like eagles; they will run and not grow weary, they will walk and not be faint. Isaiah 40:31

My flesh and my heart may fail, but God is the strength of my heart and my portion forever. Psalm 73:26

Extra Verse References on Strength:
Isaiah 40:28-30, Psalm 96:6, Psalm 105:4, Philippians 4:13, Psalm 18:32, I Corinthians 1:8-9, II Corinthians 12:9-10, Ephesians 6:10-18

Clinging to His Peace:

You will keep in perfect peace him whose mind is steadfast, because he trusts in you. Isaiah 26:3

And the peace of God, which transcends all understanding, will guard your hearts and your minds in Christ Jesus. Philippians 4:7

Extra Verse References on Peace:
Matthew 11:29-30, Philippians 4:6, John 14:27

Clinging to His Comfort:

He has made everything beautiful in its time. He has also set eternity in the hearts of men; yet they cannot fathom what God has done from beginning to end. Ecclesiastes 3:11

May your unfailing love be my comfort, according to your promise to your servant. Psalm 119:76

Extra Verse References on Comfort:
Isaiah 41:10, Isaiah 41:13, Psalm 27:1-5,
Psalm 23:1-6, Psalm 30:11-12, Psalm 27:1-14,
Matthew 5:4, I Thessalonians 4:13-18

Clinging to His Hope:

And hope does not disappoint us, because God has poured out his love into our hearts by the Holy Spirit, whom he has given us. Romans 5:5

May the God of hope fill you with all joy and peace as you trust in him, so that you may overflow with hope by the power of the Holy Spirit. Romans 15:13

Extra Verse References on Hope: Psalm 31:24, I Peter 1:21, Psalm 42:5, Psalm 119:81, Psalm 33:20-22, Proverbs 13:12, Titus 2:11-14

IN THE SUFFERING

IN THE SUFFERING

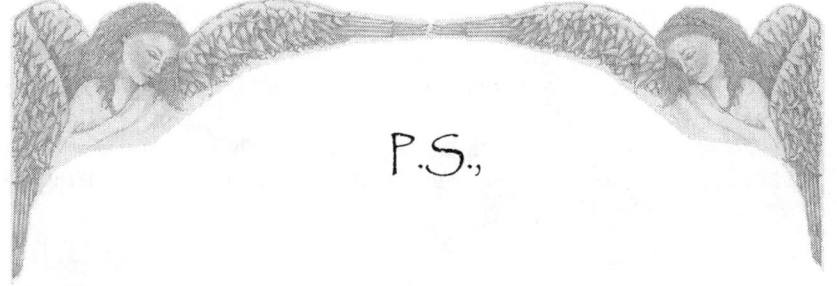

P.S.,

A few disclaimers about this book:

* The poems in this book are simple, clear and to the point in order to encourage others with God's Word.

* God is more Powerful than any comma, dash or dot.

* Even though this entire book has been edited numerous times I hope that if you find any imperfections, that it will not distract you from the main message it brings, which is Jesus our Hope!

* Some words have been capitalized intentionally in order to bring awareness to what is being said and its importance in showing reverence for who God is.

A few interesting facts about this book:

* This book is a smaller compilation of many poems from my previous book, "The Trusting Time - A Collection of Christian Poetry",

* There were 12 new poems written specifically for this book.

* One poem, Disguised Blessing, was written in January 2012 while vacationing in Red River, New Mexico a few days after ringing in the New Year.

* The following poems were written in February 2012: Drowning Faith, Bystander's Prayer, I'm Still Here, Dark Hours, Angels' Wings, Offering of Ashes, Trembling Hope, Divine Hope, He Holds You, and Eden's Hope.

* Eden's Hope was the last poem written for this book.

* Drowning Faith was a true story about someone who almost drowned while on vacation in Cancun, Mexico... That someone was me. It was my wake-up call from God to get serious about following Him. After writing this poem I cried hard for half an hour.

P.S., (cont.)

* The poems <u>Before I Miss Today</u> and <u>A Valentine of Praise</u> were both written in the year of 2000 and are making their debut in this book after spending time in a dusty desk drawer of mine.

* There are five poems that were originally song lyrics that I wrote years ago. They are: <u>If We Will Only Have Faith</u>, <u>I'm Not Afraid To Die</u>, <u>My Savior Walks By Me</u>, <u>Joy is in the Journey</u>. These can be found at the end of each section. They too, are making their debut in this book.

* I wrote <u>I'm Not Afraid To Die</u> when I was 15 years old, after visiting my great uncle while he was on his death bed when he was dying of cancer. To this day it is a favorite among my family.

* I know the tune to all four songs but only two of them ever had music notes written for them.

* The other songs were written when I was in my early 20's.

A few final acknowledgements:

*This book project has been a mixed blessing for me to write and put together. "In the Suffering" has been a vision for several years. However, having said that, God had to prepare my own heart and I had to trust Him with my own health concerns in order for me to be inspired and anointed with His Strength so that I may encourage others with this poetry.

* I also want to mention how thankful I am to God for my husband. Phil has been my manager, editor, computer tech and co-laborer during this project while accompanying me to all of my events, and through the process of getting this book published. I truly could not have done it without his sacrifice of time, encouragement and patience. God used Phil to encourage me and help me to stay focused on those dark and painful days when I was limited by my condition. So, if you ever get the chance to meet him in person you will see the better half of me. ☺

P.S., (cont.)

* In October of 2006 Phil and I lost our male cat, Kat, who was 18 years old to liver failure. Four years later in September of 2010 we lost our female cat, Buttons, who was 14 years old to kidney failure. So I can tell you that losing a pet can sometimes be as difficult as losing a person. Pets give so much unconditional love that one of these furry angels can often provide us with a form of healing in itself. These are true blessings from God. So, I must also mention the two cats I have now - Abbie and Daisy. Abbie is 11 years old and suffers from stage 2 Kidney Disease. Daisy is a little more than 1 year and she suffers from high anxiety from loud noises. These sweet furry blessings have given me the opportunity to show care and comfort to them and I can tell you they have returned the favor. In fact we call Abbie "Nurse Abbie" because she will not leave my side on the days when I don't feel well. She has recently enlisted Daisy into the same kind of training care. ☺

* Last, but certainly not least, I want to mention how blessed I am to you, the reader of this book. Yes, you! Thank you for choosing to read "this" book. Thank you for taking this book to someone in a hospital, place of care or giving it as a sympathy gift. Thank you for your servant's heart when you read it to those who are suffering or cannot read it for themselves. Thank you also to those who are recipients of this book as you allow God to comfort your heart through the poetry of Jesus' Hope, as even in your suffering your life can become poetic for Him!

One final encouragement:

There are many reasons why I write. I write because I enjoy it and I love where God takes me and my writing as I encounter His Divine Direction when I write to encourage others.

However, almost as important as why I write is "what" happens when I write. God usually gives me inspiration by first giving me a title to a poem. Then as I begin to write He will sometimes give me a vision of a faceless, nameless person who I can use for a muse.

He also will give me poems specifically to minister to my heart directly so that I may worship Him. Often these moments are so precious because I can feel Jesus to be closer than ever!

So, I would like to personally encourage you now. It may be that you could be overwhelmed with life, weak from pain or devastated from grief but Jesus can still use you. Yes YOU! Believe me if He can turn this 40 something year old woman with fibromyalgia who used to be a couch potato into a speaker and author, He can certainly do a work in your life too!

The key is to let Him set His Time for how He leads you and Glorifies His Son in your talents and abilities.

So I pray that you enjoyed (or will enjoy) this book immensely and that it will present you with the opportunity to be filled with God's Power, Strength, Comfort, Peace, and Joy as you find that quiet place to sit as Jesus' feet.

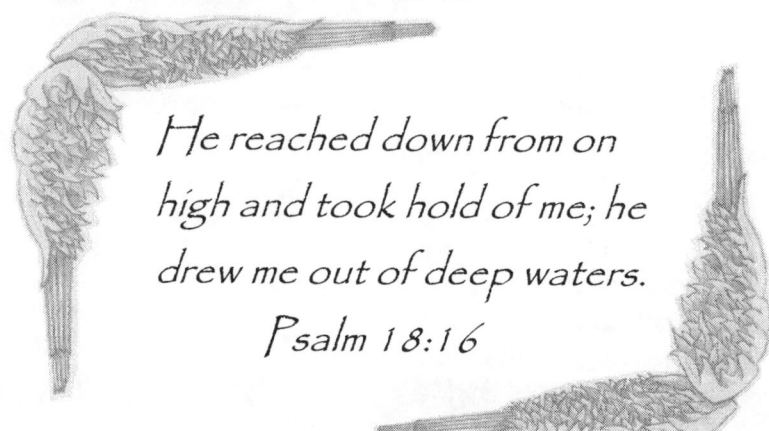

He reached down from on high and took hold of me; he drew me out of deep waters.
Psalm 18:16

Alphabetical Index of Poems

A Hope For Spring	70
A Valentine of Praise	50
Acknowledging His Holiness	viii
Angels are Here	58
Angels' Wings	57
Beautiful Lullaby	18
Before I Miss Today	48
Blessing Before Bitterness	10
Bystander's Prayer	11
Dark Hours	46
Disguised Blessing	24
Divine Hope	68
Drowning Faith	2
Eden's Hope	40
Even The Flowers Knew	71
Faith for Winter	25
Final Touches	27
Grief (The Mysterious Gift)	54
He Holds You	36
Heaven Presents "Jesus"	77
Honest Worship	80
I Cannot Feel	49
I'm Not Afraid to Die	42
I'm Still Here	33
If We Will Only Have Faith	19
In God's Hand	26
In the Clearing	34
In the Suffering	v
Joy is in the Journey	82
Just Remember	15
Just to Say	31
Look Up, Broken Hearts	6
Looking Beyond	38
My Constant	17
My Prayer of Praise	73
My Savior Walks By Me	63
Offering of Ashes	60

Alphabetical Index of Poems (continued)

Panic Attack	8
Pity Party	29
Point to Him	16
Poured Out	79
Prepare Me for Eternity	81
Sand Castles	5
Shadows	51
Sinner's Prayer	86
Storms of Life	4
Taking a Moment	74
The Crucifixion	52
The Folded Flag	55
The Great Ecstasy	75
The Heavenly King	78
The Lighthouse	12
The Main Attraction	76
The Power of Prayer	28
The Trusting Time	13
The Unanswered Prayer	30
Trapped Inside	32
Trembling Hope	62
Troubling Thoughts	9
Trust in God	14
Victorious Over All	72
Waiting on Healing	39
When Bad Things Happen	56
When The Vows Have Been Broken	7
Why Do Bad Things Happen	59
Windows of Light	35
Words Cannot Express	53

ABOUT THE AUTHOR

Jodie Mitchell is also the author of "The Trusting Time - A Collection of Christian Poetry" which was published September of 2011.

She currently lives in Crowley, Texas with her husband Phil, her two cats Abbie and Daisy and two dogs Koda and Kenai. She and her husband are the proud aunt and uncle of several nieces and nephews in Texas, Oklahoma and Australia. She and her husband presently serve at and are members of Christ Chapel Bible Church.

When she isn't writing poetry she is writing devotionals, mentoring women and praying for others. She has been involved with encouragement ministries for thirteen plus years.

To learn more about Jodie, her events, her other books or her future projects be sure and check out her website.

http://www.aprilsky.net

Words of Encouragement from Family and Friends

IN THE SUFFERING

IN THE SUFFERING

IN THE SUFFERING

IN THE SUFFERING

IN THE SUFFERING

IN THE SUFFERING

IN THE SUFFERING

IN THE SUFFERING

IN THE SUFFERING

Made in the USA
Charleston, SC
22 April 2012